Say "I DO" to LUST or LOVE

DOROTHY TATE

Say "I Do" to Lust or Love

Copyright 2019 by Dorothy Tate

ISBN 978-1-947741-45-4

Published by Kingdom Publishing, LLC
1350 Blair Drive, Odenton, MD 21113

Printed in the USA

All rights reserved. No part of this book may be reproduced, stored in retrieval system, or transmitted in any form or by any means - electronic, mechanical, photocopy, recording, or otherwise - except for brief quotations in printed reviews, without the prior written permission of the author.

Unless otherwise indicated, all Scripture quotations are taken from the King James Version (public domain).

SAY "I DO" TO LUST OR LOVE

Table of Contents

I	WHY DO WE GET MARRIED?	1
II	LOVE VS LUST	5
III	REAL TALK	13
IV	THAT WORD CALLED "FEELINGS"	15
V	"OBSTACLES"	17
VI	STAGES OF LIFE	25
VII	THE TEST	29
VIII	THE SACREDNESS OF MARRIAGE	35
IX	WHERE IS THE INTIMACY?	39
X	WHAT TO DO WHILE YOU WAIT?	41
XI	WHAT IS THAT THANG?	43
XII	EXPECTATIONS VS EXPECTANCY	45

Chapter 1
WHY DID I GET MARRIED?

In a time when marriage is on the decrease and divorce is on the rise in the church, we must go back and ask ourselves, "Why?" Didn't God institute marriage? Didn't he give us guidelines to follow before and during marriage? Then, why are our marriages failing in the church? When I first started to write this book, I thought only about marriage in the sense of husband and wife, but as time evolved, I realized that anything that you give yourself to unconditionally becomes a marriage. So, let's define marriage. Marriage is "a joining together; the state of being united to a person in a consensual and contractual relationship; fusion; merger; union or an alliance." God compared marriage to the body of Christ in Ephesians 5:22-25:

> *"For the husband is the head of the wife, even as Christ is the head of the church; and he is the Savior of the body. Therefore, as the church is subject unto Christ, so let the wives be to their own husbands in everything. Husbands love your wives, even as Christ also loved the Church,*

and gave himself for it."

Maybe it is because we marry based on the world's standard of what marriage is. We often say we marry because:

- He's good to me
- He/she is good looking
- He provides for me
- He/she loves children
- We want the same things out of life
- He promised me the world
- He/she was my first
- I couldn't imagine my life without them
- I got her pregnant, or I am pregnant, so I'm going to do the right thing
- He/she has lots of money
- He/she drives a fine car and has his/her own house
- We both love to party
- He/she is my soul mate
- My biological clock is ticking
- He treats me better than anyone I've ever dated.
- Maybe for the sake of getting married
- Loneliness

These are just a few of the reasons why we choose to get married. We adopt some of these reasons before and even after we are saved. As you can see, all of these reasons are designed to please our flesh. However, the most prevalent reason we all say we get married is for love – "We are in love."

The subject of marriage is such an important topic for me, because I have two granddaughters that I love dearly and want them to make different and better choices than I made. One of my granddaughters has obtained her M.S. degree, and the other one is in middle school, but these very beautiful young ladies, who I know will encounter many different relationships must make good decisions when developing those relationships. They must allow GOD to make them complete in him and with themselves before they say, "I do." I did not do that, and I said, "I do," because I was ready to get away from home and experience life, which was all about what pleased me. My choosing to marry based on what pleased me and not seeking GOD before marrying caused me to end up in divorce.

It is important to seek him, but also to wait for the answer. We ask God to send us our mate, and the first person that comes and emulates some of the qualities we want, we assume that they are the special one that God sent, but I've learned that Ishmael always comes before Isaac. (Selah)

This preface is something I had to study more on, whether God chooses our mate, or do we? For so long I have heard that God chooses our mate, but I started to study the word and I found that in every instance, man chose his mate. Look at Jacob, he chose Rachel and worked for years to marry her. However, even though he chose Rachel, he went to the right place to find her. He went to his own family which indicated that they had the most important thing in common. They believed the same thing. They were both believers. When we knowingly yoke ourselves with an unbeliever, we must understand that we are putting ourselves in a position of failure.

Marriage is difficult as it is, but it becomes even more difficult when we don't have the same beliefs. Now this does not mean that those qualities that he or she possess is not important, but the main ingredient must be that both parties must be believers in Christ. This is what I believe, when the vows say, "What God has joined together, let no man put asunder".

Chapter 2
LOVE VS. LUST

Well, let's examine this: "What is love?" We'll look at it from the world's perspective and God's perspective. The world characterizes love as "a deep feeling or emotion expressed by two people." This kind of love fades away based on situations and circumstances (because it is based on feelings). Love is always expressed outward whereas lust is always expressed toward one's self.

Webster, defines love as "a profoundly tender, passionate affection for another person; a feeling of warm personal attachment or deep affection as for a parent, child, or friend; sexual passion or desire." Well, this definition also describes lust. Webster defines lust as "an intense sexual desire, uncontrolled or illicit sexual desire or appetite, or delight; to yearn for." As you can see, the two definitions are somewhat synonymous, insomuch that sometimes we may think we are in love when, in reality, we are in lust.

God describes 'love' in 1 Corinthians 13:4-8:

"Love suffereth long (is patient) and is kind; love envieth not, love does not parade itself (is

> *not puffed up); does not behave unseemly; does not seek it's own; is not easily provoked (easily angered); thinks no evil; does not rejoice in iniquity (keeps no record of wrong doing) but rejoices in truth; bears all things; believes all things; hopes all things; endures all things. Love never fails."*

This kind of love is a process and requires growth and commitment. If we say we are in love, why is it so easy to give up on love? I often hear someone say, "I love him/her, but I'm not in love with them." What is the difference? There are many types of love from the ancient Greeks perspective. I'll name a few:

1. <u>Eros</u> - love of the body. Eros is based on sexual attraction. It's where the word erotica derives from. For example, you may meet someone and you immediately feel attracted or lustful toward them.
2. <u>Philia</u> - love of the mind. This kind of love exists when people share the same values and dispositions. For example, when two people get together and talk about how they understand each other and feel very comfortable with each other.
3. <u>Pragma</u> - This kind of love is longstanding between a married couple which develops over a long period of time and requires profound understanding.
4. <u>Agape</u> - This kind of love is selfless. It is unconditional.

It's the kind of love that you give without expecting anything in return. It is compassionate and giving. It's the kind of love that God wants us to have.
5. <u>Philautia</u> - this kind of love is pure selfish and seeks pleasure, fame, and wealth often leading to narcissism. Philautia love is the kind of love that takes and does not give back in return.
6. <u>Storge</u> - This is the kind of love parents naturally feel for their children. It is based on natural feelings and effortless love.

I'm sure you may have experienced one or all of these types of love, however, the kind of love God requires us to have, I feel, is a combination of Pragma and Agape – a kind of love that is selfless and grows over time.

Now let's examine why God parallels marriage to the body of Christ. Most of the time we come to him because we have tried to manage our lives on our own and we finally realize that we can't. For example, "Let's take a journey." Do you remember walking down that aisle in the church, or maybe you were in your home (wherever you were) and you were asked if you wanted to acccpt Jesus as your personal Lord and Savior? Your answer was, "Yes." You were then asked if you believed that Jesus Christ died, was buried, and rose from the grave for your sins. Again, your answer was, "Yes." Then, your new life began with renewed excitement. But as with any marriage, problems start, temptations increase, and we have a hard time staying the course. We sometimes commit spiritual adultery, where we go back to our old ways, but just like with our wedding vows, which say "in sickness and in health, forsaking all others until death do we part," we renege on our promise. However, God says in his holy word to count it all joy when we fall into various temptations and trials, because those trials and tests produce endurance. So, maybe we should allow God to fix us before we give up. Marriage is a process just like salvation.

We all say that we love God with all of our heart and soul just like we also say we will love and cherish the one we say "I DO" to. Didn't we? Or should I say, "Will we," for those who have not taken the plunge? Love is an action word and requires commitment. It requires communication—and not just one sided, where we talk and he listens, but we have to listen and let him talk. That's the same thing we must do in a marriage. We have to allow God to perfect us. This is where prayer and patience have to have its perfect will.

God describes "Lust" in Matthews 15:19 and Galatians 5:19-21:

> *"Out of the heart proceeds evil thoughts, murder, adulteries, fornications, thefts, false witness, blasphemies."*
>
> *"Now the works of the flesh are evident which*

are adultery, fornication, uncleanness, lewdness, idolatry, sorcery, hatred, contentions, jealousies, outbursts of wrath, selfish ambitions, dissentions, heresies, envy, murders, drunkenness, revelries of life."

All these glorify the flesh. All lust originates from Satan. Our society confuses love and lust. God's kind of love is directed outward toward others, not inward toward ourselves. It is utterly unselfish. This kind of love goes against our natural inclinations. This kind of love is possible only if God helps us to set aside our own desires and instincts so that we can give love while expecting nothing in return. This kind of love can only be found when we are in Christ. Thus, the closer we come to Christ, the more love we show to others.

So, I ask myself, "If we are in Christ, why are so many marriages failing in the church?" I think that we should go back and ask ourselves, "Why did we get married," or "Why do we want to get married?" I listed some of the reasons before, however, this may be a good time to ask yourself, "Why do you want to get married or Why Did You Get Married?" I wanted to get some real people to answer these questions, so I decided to take a survey of married couples as well as singles who aren't married or desire to be married in the church. I also wanted to know what would cause them to leave their spouse? Here is a copy of the survey given:

I am in the process of writing a book entitled, Say "I Do" to Lust or Love. The book will address the reasons why couples got married or if they are single, why they want to get married. Please take a few minutes to complete this brief survey and E-mail it to us. Your personal information such as your E-mail address is strictly confidential. Your name will not be used.

MARITAL STATUS
- ☐ Married
- ☐ Widowed
- ☐ Divorced
- ☐ Separated
- ☐ Never Married

WHAT IS YOUR GENDER
- ☐ Male
- ☐ Female

RELIGIOUS AFFILIATION:

IF MARRIED, DID YOU RECEIVE PRE-MARITAL COUNSELING? ☐ Yes   ☐ No

IF MARRIED, HOW LONG DID YOU DATE?
- ☐ 6 – 12 months
- ☐ 2 – 3 years
- ☐ more than 3 years

WHY DID YOU GET MARRIED? IF SINGLE, WHY DO YOU WANT TO GET MARRIED?

WHAT WOULD BE A REASON WHY YOU WOULD CONSIDER DIVORCE?

REAL TALK

These are the results of the survey taken using disaggregated data, which included interviews with singles aspiring to get married, married couples, and divorcees. Twelve percent (12%) of the couples in the age group of 50 and over were on their second marriage, but those that were still in their first marriage stayed, because it was instilled in them that you had to stay and make it work even if their partner was practicing consistent infidelity and abuse. Eighty-five percent (85%) of the couples surveyed, who were not married, stated that they wanted to get married, because they wanted to start a family and wanted to do it God's way. Most of the couples in the 50 and over category did not go through pre-marital counseling. However, those who were in the 20-30 age category did go through pre-marital counseling. All of those surveyed stated that they married because of love. All of the surveyed couples and singles said that the reasons they would consider divorce would be because of infidelity and abuse. This is where I had to pause and ask the question, "Does GOD give up on us when we turn away from him time and time again?" However, I feel the operative word is **consistently.** I'm so glad that he doesn't and that his grace and mercy is always present to take us to the next level. He takes us back, and wipe the slate clean when we ask for forgiveness. He said that he is faithful and just to forgive us of our sins and will cleanse us from all unrighteousness. WOW!!!

Chapter 4
THAT WORD CALLED "FEELINGS"

Let's examine the word, "feelings." Feelings is an emotional state or reaction, which changes based on our emotions. Well, ask yourself, can you make a life-changing decision solely based on feelings, when we know that they change? I often hear couples say, "He makes me feel…" but not realizing that feelings indeed change. Couples often end up in divorce court because the feelings have changed. I'm not saying that feelings aren't important, however, we should not base our decision to get married solely on feelings.

After talking to many singles who are dating, I would always ask them the question of why they would want to get married? The answer always began with, "He (or she) makes me 'feel…' or 'because I'm in love.'"

OBSTACLES

If we engage in sex before marriage, we are pleasing the flesh. Some Christians don't abstain from sex before marriage. Unfortunately, today, if you say that you are going to abstain, you are looked upon as being weird. Everybody wants to test drive the car before buying it, and once that union occurs, it is difficult to see. Our vision has become impaired. They can be "Jack the Ripper," and we won't care.

I heard it said by a minister one day that when two people are joined together and try to separate, it is like putting two boards together and applying the strongest glue you can find, then trying to pull it apart, you will always have uneven parts, because it will never come apart evenly. Then, we take those uneven parts to the next relationship, wanting that person to complete the parts that are missing. Why is this? We find ourselves on this journey to make or complete them, not realizing that we are only made complete in Christ. What we must do is allow GOD to take those uneven parts and make them complete and not depend on others to make us complete.

There has been so much debate in society about if we should wait to become intimate until after we are married? What does the Word say? You see, we have tried to do it according to the world's standards and what our flesh say, and we have come up short every time. Now I'm not saying that couples that engaged in intimacy before marriage don't last, however, I'm looking at marriage in its totality. Usually, when sex comes before marriage, it is difficult to see the real person. If we are real with ourselves, those of us who engaged in intimacy before marriage, our judgment was clouded and we really didn't care what their character, attitudes and actions were – we were in love. We made our decisions based on our feelings.

Then, why does everyone say they are in love, and why is it so easy to fall out of love? I know many people who proclaimed that they will love that person "until death do us part." I said the same thing, but when the trials and tribulations came, or the feelings change, the love began to fade.

I was watching a TV show one day, where this young lady was engaged to marry this man. He was sent to Iraq and was blown up by a bomb, and was badly disfigured. The question was asked, "Will you still marry him even though he's badly disfigured?" Her reply was, "I'm not marrying him for his looks, but for his heart." That was such a profound statement. We base our love on feelings, but feelings change based on circumstances.

    What about if your significant other cheats on you or does not love you the way GOD instructs him to. Do you leave? I think it is a process to learn how to love a woman based on how GOD loves the church. In order to learn how to do that, one must be taught. Most of the way we are taught to love is through society and our immediate environment. When we come to Christ, the word says that old things are passed away, behold all things become new. Think about it, we come to Christ, and ask him to come into our lives, then, life happens and we revert back to our old ways. Sometimes, we even stop allowing him to change us. We stop going to church. We stop praying, and we never pick up our Bibles. God gave us an example of spiritual adultery with the story of Hosea and Gomer in Hosea 2, where he allowed Hosea to marry a harlot (Gomer). She went out and committed adultery with many men, however, God confused the men that she was with where they did not want her anymore, so she decided to go back home to Hosea, where he was waiting with open arms. Similarly, we do the same thing as Gomer. . God gives us a free will to make our own choices; we go and do whatever pleases us, but things never go the way we plan. Consequently, when we have had enough of things not working out the way we desire, we come back to him, and of course, he is faithful to forgive us and cleanse us of all unrighteousness. He takes us back with open arms.

You see, God has given us a roadmap to follow when it comes to relationships and marriage. However, we have to allow him to change us from the inside out. It is a process. First, there is salvation, then renewal, and finally productivity. We must allow God to revive us, restore us and resurrect us. That's the way it is with marriage. I know that it is hard to fathom that you can actually love someone who treats you in a way that is not of GOD or who cheats on you, but does God stop loving us based on what we do or don't do? I know by now that you are saying that you are not God, however, this is where we have to allow God to change us (or them). Usually it is us. The operative word is lifestyle. If we continually cheat, then we are not changing. However, GOD did give us a reason for divorce which is sexual immorality. Notwithstanding, I believe that God forgives us for anything, as long as we come to him, and confess our sins. He is faithful and just to forgive us of our sins and to cleanse us from all unrighteousness. Then we must repent – not by just saying, "I'm sorry," but by going in a different direction, resisting the devil when he comes, and then allowing God to renew our minds. This is why I believe it is so important to look deep inside the cup before getting married. Everything is time tested.

This brings up the question of love at first sight. I personally believe that there can be a strong attraction at first sight which makes you want to begin the process of looking inside the cup, however, getting to know the person takes time. How do you get to know a person? Everyone is putting on their best face and presenting the best picture of themselves when you first meet. This is the expectancy phase, where it's all about getting to know each other, laughing, and sharing, then, if-and when intimacy occurs, our relationship moves from expectancy to expectations where it's all about what you did or are expected to do. Now you are expected to perform in a way that meets my expectations. This changes the whole dynamics of the relationship. The real person slowly starts to show up, then we go through this phase of trying to change him/her to meet our expectations. When we find that we can't change them, we become disappointed, angry, and sometimes disillusioned. People don't change unless they see the need to change, not because you don't like something about them.

    I think that so many of us have these high expectations of what marriage is, so when things happen, we are ready to throw in the towel, by cheating, fighting or just ignoring the problems. Now, don't get me wrong, high expectations are good when getting married, however, they should also be realistic. You are taking two different people with different upbringings and ideologies and infusing them together.

    Another reason I think that our marriages are

failing is because (as I stated before) we don't give ourselves time to get to know the person (in other words, taking the time to look inside the cup). You must admit when you meet someone, you usually deal with the superficial stuff like what do you like to do? Where do you work, and where do you live, etc.? We never ask the real questions like, "What are your short and long term goals?" Asking questions like this one will give you an indication of where they are going to take you? If a man has no goals, then he can't lead you anywhere, simply because he doesn't even know where he is going. This applies to women also. They have to know where they are going in order to follow.

Most Christians look at the fact that they attend church as a prerequisite for choosing a mate. Well, I'm here to tell you that attending church definitely isn't a barometer for measuring whether a person is the one for you or not. There are many men and women who attend church, but they are not on a journey to become the church. See, I believe that we are the church and if we don't deal with the issues in our own lives and allow God to change us, we are uniting two vessels together looking for the other to complete us. I've learned that there is no man or woman that can complete you. You can only be complete in Christ. Flaws, character and integrity can only be shaped and changed first by admitting that there are flaws and then allowing GOD to change them. Dealing with the issues in your own life is crucial. If you are dealing with low self-esteem, jealousy, envy, anger, childhood issues, past abuse, hurt, insecurities, and all the issues that describe lust, etc. and you get married, those issues don't go away, they are only compounded. You then look for the other person to make it better and they can't.

According to Revelations 19:7, which states, "Let us be glad and rejoice, and give honor to him; for the marriage of the Lamb is come, and his wife hath made herself ready." This passage is not gender bias. We must make ourselves ready for the coming of our Savior, just like we must make ourselves ready for our earthly bride/husband. This means we must prepare ourselves spiritually, financially, physically, emotionally and intellectually before marriage. It is an ongoing process.

Another issue that is critical to the demise of marriage is Money. The bible says that the love of money is the root of all evil. If the person you are marrying has problems with money management and does not understand how money works, then you have a big problem on your hands. For example, if he/she loves to buy expensive clothes and shoes, etc. when you are dating, don't expect it to change when you get married. If he/she is very frugal with money when you are dating that doesn't change when you get married; it is only compounded. There must be goals set when it comes to money. If you don't set goals as it relates to money, then you end up in debt and having nothing when you really need it. We have to learn how to make our money work for us and not just us working for our money.

I've found that in our community, creating family wealth is a problem. First of all, some of us are not taught how to make our money work for us. We are constantly trying to make ends meet, so when we get money it goes on survival, which makes it difficult to save.

I remember my grandmother, who worked as a maid, always had money tied up in a dirty handkerchief, and we always had all of the necessities of life. I remember asking her why she used a dirty handkerchief. She replied, "If I accidentally dropped it, no one would pick it up." I look back now and wonder how did she accomplish it on the amount of money she was bringing in as a maid, but she did. I know the cost of living has changed, however, what if we just put back $25 per month, we would always have something. This is one thing that has to be discussed prior to marriage. We must also look at their credit history, not to condemn them, but to give us an idea of how they prioritize. We also must make sure that our own credit history is a priority. Now, that does not mean that we must have perfect credit, however, we do need to make sure we have a plan and the means to take care of our financial responsibilities.

Chapter 6
STAGES OF LIFE

One thing for sure that I've learned is that there are stages in our lives, and our thinking is different in each stage. For example, when I was in my teens and twenties (20's), I wanted to get away from my parents and do my own thing. I felt that I knew all I needed to know to make it. I felt like I had found Mr. Right and we were going to live happily ever after. Little did I know that I wanted to get married based on my own lusts and desires. I thought that the love I had would be enough to change him, but little did I know that the change had to begin in me. If I had allowed God to change me, I probably would not have married him. We marry people based on where we are in our lives. It's not until things begin to change in our lives that we are able to see clearly what kind of mate we need.

I remember the late Dr. Myles Monroe saying, "We should marry based on purpose." What does that mean? It means that both of us should, first of all, know our own purpose for being on earth, and the person we choose should know his/her purpose, or at least, on a quest to find out. I did not know my purpose before

I got married, neither did I know his. We both were caught up in the feelings. When the feelings changed, we changed. Neither of us gave ourselves a chance to get to know who the other person really was and allow God to fix those parts that had been damaged by life's circumstances. I did not give myself the opportunity to experience and enjoy my singleness at that stage in my life. stead, I got married, and began having children. I wanted to learn more about this stage of life, so I started to research what happens to the brain in our 20's, since this is where I found that most of us feel like we are ready for marriage, and society tells us that this is a good age to get married and begin a family.

What I learned is, according to Health Coach Institute, research on the brain shows that contrary to what we once thought, we don't suddenly develop an adult brain as soon as we leave our teens. Neurologically, it seems we continue to develop through our adolescence and well into our twenties.

When you are in your 30's, your ideas and plans seem to become more focused. If you do not allow yourself a chance to live on your own, gain independence, travel or begin to achieve all of the things you want to accomplish before you get married, there may be regrets. Once you get married and begin having a family, then try to do those things you missed, there can be problems. There are always exceptions.

Women, there are clues that we must look for

when looking inside the cup.

1. How does he handle crisis? Does he complain about them or does he pray about it?
2. Is he/she on a quest to become the church or do they just attend church?
3. Is he a provider?
4. Does he have a protective instinct as it relates to you?

Women find it difficult to turn from a man and stop demanding that he meet their needs, provide security, protect their identity and return to GOD. Men, on the other hand, find it hard to turn from the works of their hands, move from their own quest for power, security and significance and return to GOD.

Chapter 7
THE TEST

    I tried so hard to complete this book, but I became stalled, experienced writer's block and could not write anything. What I learned is that GOD wanted me to experience the book. I had to be tested in the very thing that I wanted to tell others about. I was looking at this book theoretically and with the understanding of what the word says about LOVE and Lust, but I had to live it first, and believe me I did! It was not until now that I am able to begin putting all of my thoughts down and the words are beginning to flow.

    After I truly accepted Christ, I was alone for over 30 years before meeting someone. Because I know Christ, I felt like I was ready and believed he was the one. Well, I had to see that just because you feel he is the one, he had to see that I was the one for him, too.

    The first thing to keep you from saying, "I do" to lust is to define what is that thing that you want so much in a relationship? We want so much for someone to take care of us and make us feel special. However, we must realize that sometimes we are more interested in the preparation of getting married and feeling the excitement, that we don't take the time to get to truly know the person we want to marry (LUST). I know that it has been said that you don't get to know a person until you live with them, but there are ways to find out some things before you get married.

We went through pre-marital counseling where we talked about money management, family matters and personal flaws; we even prepared our home, etc. We even attended church together. Unfortunately, I didn't let GOD make him the spiritual leader I needed. On the contrary, I attempted to make him that leader. I urged him into prayer or studying the Word. I saw the signs of him needing to be healed in an area of his life that would cause problems in the marriage. Although I didn't ignore it and complained about it, I was not going to let it become a deal-breaker for us, because I felt that since we were in church together it would change. I soon realized that being in church does not mean that that person is for you, and people don't change unless they recognize the area in their lives that need to be changed, and are ready and willing to make the change. It is so important for each person to establish a relationship with Christ and for that relationship to be time tested.

It is so important to let GOD choose our mate. However, after much meditation, I asked myself if this indeed is a true statement? Does GOD choose our mate or do we? I went back to the word and saw an example of Jacob and Rachel. Jacob chose Rachel and not Leah. However, he went to his family's bloodline to get her, which indicates that we must be equally yoked.

I'm reminded of a TV show entitled, "Married at First Sight." I was introduced to this show by my aunt and cousin. They urged me to watch it. I said that I felt the show was stupid, because to me, it takes time to get to know a person, and to marry someone whom you just met was unrealistic. Nonetheless, I decided to watch the show, and became intrigued with the process. The show was considered to be an extreme experiment. The experiment lasts for several weeks. The couples could decide at the end of the so-called marital experiment whether or not they wanted to stay married or get a divorce. The couples were paired by four specialists, consisting of a sexologist, a pastor, a psychologist and a sociologist. These specialists used scientific matchmaking methods to determine the selection of each couple, who had not met and had no contact until they are married. These couples are asked to get to know each other based on their commonalities rather than just physical attractions. The couples move in with each other and begin the process of trying to get to know each other.

On one episode, three of the couples remained celibate with each other while getting to know each other, however, one of the couples had a physical attraction from the beginning and decided to consummate their marriage. At the end of the process three of the four couples decided to remain married, but one decided to get a divorce. This show was an example of how the world's system shows us how to choose our mates.

One thing that fascinated me about the show was that the marriage came first, then the couples went on a journey to learn everything about each other after being married. I have considered starting a marriage university where singles and couples could take courses in each area that they may face in marriage before getting married. The final course would be a prerequisite for getting married.

Nowadays, there are many dating sites and TV shows to help us find our mate. It is imperative that we examine the word to determine What GOD says about finding and keeping a mate.

1. A godly mate should be sought only when it is certain that marriage will achieve the purposes God has for our lives.
2. If we want to have a godly mate, we must wait for God's time.
3. If we want a godly mate, we must look in the right place.
4. If we want a godly mate, we must look for godly qualities.
5. He who finds a godly mate should be willing to heed the counsel of older and wiser Christians.

6. He who wants a godly mate must be willing to put emotional feelings last.

For example, in Genesis 24:67, Isaac brought Rebekah into his mother's tent, and took her, and she became his wife, and he loved her, and Isaac was comforted after his mother's death. Notice love came last, not first. Isaac learned to love his wife in time, which leads me to a principle which many Christian counselors often stress: Romantic love is never the basis for marriage, however, marriage is the basis for romantic love.

Romantic love is a wonderful emotional feeling, but it will never sustain a marriage. Don't put yourself in a situation where romantic love can grow until you are certain that you want it to grow. Everything in our society runs contrary to this principle. The kind of love that God requires us to have is a process and it takes time. Love is a gift from God.

Chapter 8
THE SACREDNESS OF MARRIAGE

According to the word of GOD in the Old Testament, we become married when we "go into each other," i.e. have sex. When the man chose his wife, they were not considered married until they consummated the marriage, however, there was an espousal period. The espousal period was very sacred in the Bible. In our culture, we call this the engagement. Once you chose the woman you wanted to marry and went to the father to gain permission, the woman had to remain pure until the marriage. Otherwise, she could be killed if she had sex with anyone else.

We get married for all kinds of reasons and we get divorced for so many trivial reasons. My focus is on the church. We have to start looking at marriage the way GOD intended it to be. I often wondered why GOD compared marriage to the body of Christ. There is a real example of this in the book of Hosea.

As I mentioned before, God told Hosea to marry a harlot, which was an analogy of how our relationship is with God. Gomer went out and had several affairs. Hosea stayed home and took care of the children, however, God ended up confusing her partners which was an example of how the world rejected Jesus. The men rejected Gomer so she decided to go back to Hosea. Take a walk with me in your mind: You meet someone you love and you decide you want to spend the rest of your life with them. You decide to walk down the aisle with him and take vows that you will love them until death do you part, but then you start to have the "for better or for worse" problems and you decide to terminate the relationship and walk away. Well, isn't that what we do when we come to Christ? We come to the altar and ask him to come into our lives. We vow to live our lives according to his WORD, then when we face various trials and tribulations, we walk away and go back to our former relationship with the world.

That's what God was showing us with the story of Hosea and Gomer. God was illustrating how the children of Israel left their husband (Christ) and started to intermingle with the world. However, it shows through Hosea the love God has for us, because when she returned, he was faithful to forgive her and restore her back. I know we may be saying that this kind of love can only be done by Jesus, but it is the kind of love that God requires us to have. Now, God does give us an out when we get married, it is for sexual immorality, but nowadays we divorce for any reason.

That's why it is so important to go through extensive premarital counseling. Although premarital counseling is not a guarantee, it encourages us to allow God to not only be a part of our relationship before we say, "I Do," but to continue to make him the center of our relationship afterwards as well. By doing this, we can have the marriage that God designed for us.

Chapter 9
WHERE IS THE INTIMACY?

What is intimacy? It is defined as "close familiarity, or friendship, togetherness, affection, warmth, confidence." Intimacy is not just physical.

This is an area that I see missing in a lot of relationships in the church. Now, I know this can be a challenging statement, however, the intimacy seems to change after marriage with some marriages. Why is this? I have been able to see examples of intimacy with some couples. I had the opportunity to meet a husband and wife who had been married for 47 years. They were still touching and kissing in public. They loved dancing with each other. It was so amazing. How do you maintain the intimacy, the closeness, the warmth, the friendship and the affection?

I also had the opportunity to see that with my mom and my stepfather. My stepfather recently passed, but before he passed, I saw a true example of what the word says to us in Ephesians 5:22-23, which states, "Husbands love your wife as Christ loved the church and gave himself for her."

My father had COPD and for the last days of his

life, he had to be on 24-hour oxygen. This happened during Christmas and my mother always loved to have the lights on around the house. My mother and I went out to try and hook up the lights, with no success. We went upstairs first, and when I came back downstairs, this is when I noticed my father was having shortness of breath. I tried to get him to slow down his breathing while increasing his oxygen. His oxygen level was down to 30%. I asked him what was wrong and what caused his breathing to become so labored? He said to me, "I had gone out, climbed upon a ladder to try and connect the lights up around the house." I was flabbergasted! He had put his life in jeopardy at the expense of pleasing my mom. He was willing to die in order to serve her. Isn't that what Christ did for us? That scripture came to mind. For years I watched my dad serve my mother every meal on a tray. This was a true example of selfless love. They were married for 47 years.

Chapter 10
WHAT TO DO WHILE YOU WAIT

I know that most singles who are wanting and waiting to get married, have a hard time with the word, "wait." There are so many ways that society has formulated to help one find a mate, but what they don't have is a method to help us determine what to do while we wait. We get so involved in the seeking and searching of a mate, but then when they finally com, we are just like the ten virgins who did not take the time to make sure they had enough oil in their lamps; for when the bridegroom came for them, they were ill-prepared.

So, what do we do while we wait? According to Revelation 19:7-8, which says, "Let us be glad and rejoice, and give honor to him, for the marriage of the Lamb is come, and his wife hath made herself ready. And to her was granted that she should be arrayed in fine linen, clean and white, for the linen is the righteousness of saints." Since we all are the bride of Christ, this scripture is not gender biased. This says that we should prepare ourselves spiritually, physically, emotionally, financially, etc., so that when our mate comes we can rejoice and be glad.

Most of the time, as I have stated before, one of the major reasons why couples get divorced is because we don't take the time to look inside the cup. Another reason we get divorced is because we don't allow God to complete us in him and we depend on our mate to complete us. We must ask ourselves the question, "Am I complete in him?" Have we allowed GOD to deal with us, with our past hurts, insecurities, fears and doubts? Have we set goals for ourselves and are consistently on the path for achieving those goals?

Chapter 11
WHAT IS THAT THANG?

We spend most of our lives seeking for that "thang" that we think is going to complete us. Is it a husband, job, car, house, money, etc.? It always amazes me that when we get "that thang," then we move on to the next thang. There is no "thang" (or person) that is able to satisfy the need in us except Christ. When we finally realize that there is nothing that will satisfy that need in us except Jesus, we should not continue seeking that thang. It always amazes me how God blesses us with something and before we can praise him for that blessing, we are on to something else.

Why do we marry for the wrong reasons? One reason I have surmised is that it starts with low self-esteem. Previously, I did a workshop on "What's Your Worth?" I gave each person a paper doll and told a story using a lot of negative words. Every time the person heard a negative word, they were to tear a piece of the paper doll. After that, I told the same story, but this time using positive words. The group was then asked to try and put the doll back together using tape or glue. They saw how difficult it was to reassemble the paper doll, because they had so many uneven parts and each part left ridges. The illustration showed them how words, family and life issues shaped their lives. It also showed them how hard it was to put themselves back together. We spend our lives trying to fix those parts that are broken and consequently choose people in our lives that we feel can fix those parts. Unfortunately, when we finally realize that they cannot fix those parts, we become disappointed and hurt and end up leaving or finding other ways to satisfy that need. Some people turn to drugs, alcohol, other people, religion (instead of relationship with God), sex, etc. Until that need is fulfilled, the cycle will continue. The only way that need can be fulfilled is through first submitting it to Jesus and being honest, because he already knows. Then, we must allow him to fix it, which sometimes can be very painful, but it is worth the pain to be free.

Chapter 12
EXPECTATION VS. EXPECTANCY

I found that we go into relationships with many expectations instead of expectancies. You see, according to William Young, the author of the book, "The Shack," the word, "expectations" is a noun and "expectancy" is a verb. Let's use the word, "friendship," for an example. When you see your friend, there is an expectancy of being together, of laughing, talking and reminiscing. You see, expectancy has no concrete definition. It is alive and dynamic. If expectancy changes to expectation, spoken or unspoken, expectations has entered into the relationship and now you are expected to perform in a way that meets our needs. Our loving friendship rapidly deteriorates into a dead thing with rules and requirements. It's no longer about you and your friend. Rather, it alters into what friends are supposed to do, or the responsibilities of a good friend. Responsibilities and expectations are the basis of guilt, shame and judgment, and they provide the essential framework that promotes performance as the basis for a friendship. When this happens, you start to pull away from that particular friend, because, even unknowingly, the friendship has taken on a whole new meaning. Resentment starts to creep in.

Our expectations sometimes come from how we were raised and our environment. Most of the time our expectations come from what we have seen or experienced in our lives. If we don't have any examples of a good marriage in Christ, we have nothing to draw from. Some experiences that I had which could have played a factor in me having superficial expectations were being a single parent and not growing up with my father and never seeing how a man was supposed to treat a woman. Quite naturally, with experiences like these, a person will pick up different ideas from their peers or what they may see on television. Ultimately, we take those ideas into our relationship and expect the other person to fulfill those unwarranted and unrealistic ideas that we picked up and have envisioned in our lives. This is what happens to many couples when they get married.

Before we were married, we survived on expectancy, where we couldn't wait to see the other person and spend time with them. Then, we get married and expectations start to creep in, and we no longer get excited about being together, because now, the other person is not meeting our expectations. Suddenly, we become disillusioned with our marriage, start to argue, pull away and try to get those needs met in other ways. As I have stated before, there is no person on Earth that can fulfill all of our needs. They can meet some of our physical needs, and even some of our emotional needs, but ultimately the only one that can meet our needs completely is Christ.

It takes two complete persons in Christ to go through the process of being married.. The first thing we need to do in order to even begin the process of being married is to accept the Lord Jesus Christ into our lives, allow him to guide us daily in how to be married, which takes total submission to HIS will. We must then submit our flaws, needs and desires to him; allow him to change us and not depend upon the other person to fix us.

In order to marry based on love, we must first love ourselves because the word of God says that the greatest commandment is to love God with all of our hearts, mind, soul and strength, AND to love our neighbor as OURSELVES. We must love ourselves.

Well, the way you love you, is the way you will end up loving your spouse. So first, let God teach us how to love him, then through loving him, you will learn to love yourself. From this process, you can learn best how to love your spouse. When you try to love someone else and you don't love yourself, you are continuously looking for that person to love you. People love you the way you love yourself. Don't let lust be your guide in marriage. Let us allow God to guide us and teach us how to love so that we can truly have the kind of marriage he desires for us. This way, we can finally say, "I Do," to Love instead of Lust.

www.ingramcontent.com/pod-product-compliance
Lightning Source LLC
Chambersburg PA
CBHW052126110526
44592CB00013B/1773